AF578536

HOW TO INCREASE YOUR SALES IN 30 DAYS OR LESS

Sales Success That Will Boost Your Market Evaluation

BY

VICTOR MAX

Copyright ©□ 2022

All Right Reserved

Contents

INTRODUCTION

Everyday, several folks participate in innumerable sales transactions across the world. This creates a continuing flow of assets and forms the backbone of the associated economies. The sales of products and services among a retail market are an additional common sort of sales transaction; the sales of investment vehicles within the money markets are thought about extremely refined worth exchanges.

A sale may be completed as a part of the operation of a business among a market or a vesture merchandiser still as between people. Things purchased through a cut-rate sale would be thought about a procurement between people whereas getting a private vehicle from an automobile franchise would represent a procurement between a personal and a business.

Sales may be completed between businesses, like once one raw materials supplier sells offered materials to a business that uses the materials to supply commodities.

Making a procurement needs you to be convincing and sincere, it needs you to create a reference to your client, and most significantly, it needs you to understand along with your client's wants. A good employee makes a troublesome job appear as if it is a simple job. It needs toil, persistence, and also the ability to urge up when you've been knocked down.

MAXIMIZING YOUR SALES

Whether that's a service, a product, or a chunk of valuable information everybody has one thing they will sell.

But the sole manner a business succeeds is by earning customers and growing sales from that service, product, or information.

You can't simply hope somebody can come across your product and get it, though.

An increase in sales doesn't simply happen, it's the results of thoughtful sales ways that are planned and dead. So as to extend sales, you've got to extend the quantity of consumers you're marketing to, enhance what you're marketing, and improve your electronic messaging.

If you'll be able to improve each step of your sales method by even a bit, you'll be able to increase sales by plenty.

1
INCREASE SALES BY INCREASING LEADS

One powerful way to increase sales is to extend leads.

The additional folks that have access to your purpose of sales system or place of business means that additional folks have the chance of shopping for you and increasing your profits.

Here are a few ways in which to get additional results in boosting sales and increase profits.

- **Obviously Outnumber Your Client**

First, you would like to grasp the United Nations agency you're targeting. United Nations agency is that the one that would presumably get your product and pass away immediately?

Create an associate avatar of that client. Raise yourself specific questions about them:

How precious are they?
Are they male or female?
Do they need children?
How much cash do they make?
What are they interested in?
What are their priorities?
Knowing the answers to those queries can assist you produce additional correct electronic messaging around your product and target the proper audience in your selling efforts.

◻ Define Your Client To Extend Sales

Identify the matter you're making an attempt to unravel.

When you're certain, you've got a transparent understanding of your ideal client, their pain points, and their needs, then you'll be able to perceive however you'll be able to facilitate.

What drawback will your product or service solve? How will it address the pain of your customer?

If you have got to know your client properly, and savvy your product helps solve their drawback, they'll pass away from you. If, however, the client you have outlined doesn't have this drawback, they won't obtain your product.

All nice success and everyone's nice fortunes come back from serving folks with what they need and they are willing to pay higher than somebody else. By adopting a help instead of a sales outlook, you'll be able to perceive a way to serve folks higher and supply unbelievable client service.

- ## Try To Reach Resolute Your Customers

If worry of rejection is what's keeping you from beginning sales conversations, which might be the explanation why such a big amount of folks do not sell their product. What you have got to try and do is to succeed in reselling your customers as quickly as possible, either by call or customized email.

The goal is to follow reproval folks, not essentially to visualize results although which will happen.

When you try this, you'll not solely become fearless of finding the phone, however you'll additionally find out how folks answer your pitch and become a higher employee attributable to it. Simply make sure to not sacrifice the standard of the decision simply to visualize it off your list.

You never understand how a UN agency might grow to be a paying client.

- Utilize Ads

Sometimes it is smart to pay cash so as to create cash, however it doesn’t need to take heaps. With the correct ad, even a tiny low budget is often effective and increases leads. you only need to understand the UN agency your audience is, wherever you would like to succeed in them, and for a long time. contemplate Google, Facebook, and Instagram ads, Amazon's, looking on wherever your client is at.

When utilizing ads as a part of your strategy to extend sales, it's an honest plan to run tests. Ad tests can assist you learn the method of making ads, assist you to perceive your audience, and guarantee your budget is placed in sensible use.

2

INCREASE SALES BY CONNECTING ALONG WITH YOUR CUSTOMERS

Establishing trust along with your customers is essential to ultimately persuading them to get what you're commercialism. Even in a more and more virtual world, there are many ways to attach along with your customers, establish trust, and gain influence.

Here are a few ways to enhance sales hereby connecting along with your customers.

▫ Maximize Social Media

Social media may be a free area wherever you'll be able to connect along with your customers daily. If your client is mistreated by social media, you would like to be mistreated by social media. This can keep you high in mind after they contemplate what they need or ought to obtain.

As you employ social media posts, like photos, videos, and captions, make sure to produce valuable information; avoid talking at your customers and instead try and teach them or justify one thing to them that's in line with what your product or service is all regarding.

You can additionally use social media as an area to indicate proof that your product or service really works, like before and when stats, photos, or testimonials further as videos of the merchandise or service at work.

Don’t forget to retort to comments and answer queries. This can be incredible thanks to facilitating sales to new leads.

Remember to be friendly and colloquial as you approach your customers and potential customers during this area. If you employ it properly, you'll be able to establish trust and increase your leads.

◻ Promote Information

Everyone loves an honest deal, and after they want they need the within scoop on an forthcoming sale, or receive early access, your customers can develop larger trust in and loyalty to your business. they will even obtain additional attributable to it.

This doesn’t solely select sales and special offers. Keep current and repeat customers within the loop with forthcoming launches and news too, and soon, they’ll develop an unconditional interest within the business.

◻ Maintain Relationships

Once a client, continuously a client this could be your saying if you would like to find out a way to increase sales in business.

Once a client has purchased your product, it shouldn't be the top of your interaction with them.

Focus on maintaining a robust relationship along with your client by creating them feel valued in order that they stick around, and obtain others to become customers further. A forever client can do additional for your business than ten one-time customers.

◻ Implement A Referral Program

Everyone desires to feel appreciated, and a good thanks to build your customers feel valued is to reward them for referring to their friends and relations.

Not solely can this facilitate maintaining your relationship along with your customers however it'll additionally assist you gain new leads UN agencies are additional possible to get as a result of they received an instantaneous referral, all with none extra effort on your half.

3

INCREASE SALES BY PROVIDING WORTH MAKE CUSTOMERS FEEL VALUED TO EXTEND SALES

At the end of the day, you're commercialism, one thing that gives worth to somebody else in how, shape, or form.

If your potential customers don't understand what that worth is, they won't obtain it from you. By lightness why and the way your product offers worth, you'll be able to boost sales and additionally inspire confidence. This can be a way to sell a product.

- Place A Reward

One way to assist potential customers see the worth your business provides is to present them one thing very nice for complimentary. Freebies are a good thanks to build trust with heat leads UN agencies aren’t quite able to purchase your actual product. When they get a preview of what you provide, they're going to be more likely to shop for it.

This gift is often a style of your actual product or service, or it is often one thing that supplements it. no matter what your gift is, guarantee it's valuable in and of itself; this can be however you earn the trust of your leads, get them excited for what’s next, and drive an actual sale.

▫ Sell The Profit, Not The Merchandise

People don't obtain products, they obtain the results that the merchandise can offer. Remember the assistance not sell mentality once promoting and commercialism your product or service can assist you concentrate on its advantages.

When you obtain to initially facilitate others, it comes across as additional real instead of aggressive and simply wanting to create a fast buck. Plus, it reminds your customers of the worth your product or service provides.

4

INCREASE SALES BY PRESENTING THE MERCHANDISE EFFECTIVELY

Presenting your product effectively can assist you increase sales by increasing conversion rates, the speed at which you change leads into paying customers.

Your conversion rate is the life of the effectiveness of your sales efforts. So as to assist drive conversion rates, you would like to figure on developing your dig in a transparent, effective method. Here's a way to do this.

- Develop Your Competitive Advantage

The odds are unit smart that you're not the sole one commercializing your specific product or service. Therefore, it's crucial to be able to justify the advantages or results your customers can receive from getting your product or service that they'll not get once getting the merchandise or service of your contender.

In order to develop your competitive advantage, you wish to grasp what else is out there.

What area unit your competitors' claims? What area unit the advantages they're selling? However, is what you're giving different?

You ought to be able to specify why individuals should select your product or service over others on the market if you would like to be growing sales.

◻ Pick The Proper Value

The price you set for your product or service is vital. Not solely will it have an effect on your profits, however it additionally affects the perceived price of what you're giving.

Before you identify it, you wish to completely perceive the prices related to manufacturing the merchandise and acquire a grievance of what your ideal client would be willing to procure. you furthermore might have to recognize what your competitors are unit charging for similar merchandise or services.

One of the most effective sales ways is to beat your competitor's value, however, you furthermore might have to create cash. If you'll create your product to appear superior to your competitors, you'll be able to charge the next value. Keep this in mind and use it to assist you set the proper value.

- ## Make Sure Your Electronic Communication Is Obvious

Have clear electronic communication to extend sales.

When it involves learning the way to market a product or service, clarity is crucial. Choose one to two key advantages that your product offers and state them clearly all told the content that's a part of your sales and selling strategy. This may make sure the story you're telling regarding your product is aligned across all of your selling channels and your customers recognize precisely what it's you're commercialism.

- ## Market Content On Multiple Channels

As a part of your in progress strategy to extend sales, you must be frequently seeking artistic ways to boost your advertising and promotional efforts to succeed in new customers.

There are such a large number of mediums out there together with Twitter, Instagram, Facebook, LinkedIn, TikTok, Youtube, email, blogs, podcasts, even ancient print materials like magazines and newspapers which will get your message and products to the proper audience.

5

INCREASE THE QUANTITY AND SIZE OF TRANSACTIONS

You already recognize that it's necessary to retain your customers and maintain your relationships with them, therefore once you have got them, however does one get them to shop for from you again?

This is a very important question to raise yourself once developing a sales strategy.

If you'll increase the frequency of purchase by one-tenth, you'll increase your sales and so profits by an equivalent proportion.

Here are some ways that you'll get your customers to shop for you a lot of often, and get a lot of normally.

- Stay Prime Of Mind

How did your customers realize you within the first place? Does one have their email? Do they follow you on social media? Did you meet face to face? however ever it absolutely was they found you, still use that methodology of communication to remain prime of mind.

Send out regular emails with offers, highlighted merchandise, or useful info. Still post consistent content on your social media accounts. Decide them to examine it and see if there's the rest they have or however they're enjoying their purchase.

You want to be the primary business they think about once they would like what you sell.

Stay prime of mind to extend sales.

- Apply Increasing Savings

In order to induce your customers to shop for a lot, take into account applying discounts to larger purchases, like free shipping on orders over $80.

When promoting a buying deal, take into account giving an inflated quantity off on larger purchases, i.e., three hundredth off orders of $300 or a lot of and half-hour off orders of $600 or a lot of.

The a lot they pay, the a lot of discounts they receive.

- Look For Opportunities To Upsell Customers

You should frequently be trying to find ways to up-sell customers so they get a lot on every occasion.

What merchandise or services can complement what they're already purchasing?

Once you prove your price and have loyal customers, they'll doubtless say affirmative to you a lot of and a lot of.

- Raise Your costs

In some cases, raising your costs could be a viable possibility that would facilitate generating a lot of sales, when making an attempt several of the opposite sales ways on this list. you must totally analyze your prices, compare your costs to your competition, and perceive the demand for your product or service first moreover.

In several ways, though, you'll raise your costs by five or ten (%) percent while not experiencing any market resistance. If your merchandise and services are unit of fine quality and your individuals are unit friendly and useful, a tiny low increase in your overall costs won't drive your customers away.

6

INCREASE SALES BY FINANCE IN YOURSELF

Improving your ability to sell and convert interested prospects into paying customers is one of the foremost necessary stuff you will do to spice up sales. There are several components of the commercialism method and rising in even one in every of them will have a dramatic impact on your results.

- Attend Sales Trainings

Some individuals are naturally smart at selling; they'll simply connect with a client, realize the ground, perceive their wishes, and persuade them to buy their product. These skills don’t return simply to everybody, though.

In fact, the bulk of salespeople have to be compelled to learn, practice, and hone these skills over time to become winning. Even though you've worked arduous to become the employee you're nowadays, you're never done learning.

Sales coaching will open your mind to new opportunities others have seen success with, permit you an opportunity to network with alternative inventive salespeople, and even generate new leads or partnerships.

▫ Learn How To Barter

For some purpose in your sales journey, you're planning to run into somebody World Health Organization needs a lower cost or further profit, or a scenario where you'll have to be compelled to compromise.

Learning a way to hash out can't solely assist you improve your relationship together with your customers however may also assist you drive a lot of sales. The most effective negotiators look out for his or her customer's best interests and realize an answer that works for each party.

▫ Develop A Prospecting Strategy

The best salespeople have a thought to develop the best quality and amount of prospects which will and can get inside an inexpensive amount of your time.

Prospecting is a vital part of winning sales ways and one thing you would like to place if you would like to extend sales.

7

OUTSELL COMPETITION BY PROCESS YOUR NICHE

If you're a business owner, I feel you'll agree that the market is saturated with businesses that are unit commercialism, similar products or services, regardless of the business. As a result of this, you will notice your business is troubled to contend against the numerous peers in your business.

You may struggle to achieve customers, increase sales, rank in search terms, or simply struggle to induce your name out there.

This is an incredible headache to ablaze and drive business homeowners because it could seem like regardless of what quantity cash, time, and a focus they place into their sales or selling, they're not seeing a comeback on their efforts.

If this looks like you, you ought to contemplate the process of redefining your niche. This can build all the distinctions you would like to outsell your competition. This is often particularly necessary for little businesses.

What Is A Niche?

A niche is outlined as a specialized phase of the marketplace for a specific product or service. Within the business sphere, a distinct segment could be a specialized or centered space of a broader market that companies will differentiate themselves from the competition.

Niche also can mean no price war. This is often as a result of many house owners being tempted to differentiate their business by giving the bottom costs within the market.

What they're doing is setting themselves up for bankruptcy as a result of anyone will undercut them on worth. If they still attempt to supply the bottom costs, they place themselves into a contest on worth that leads them to no profits.

The key's to tell yourself apart from the competition by giving one thing distinctive. You'll do that by processing your distinctive commercialism Proposition, or Unique Selling Price.

8

DEFINING YOUR DISTINCTIVE COMMERCIALISM PROPOSITION

This will need a touch of analysis on your half. We advise viewing your competition's web site, marketing, social media, etc. Then raise yourself these questions:

What does one provide that they don't?
What method is unit higher than your competitors?
Is your client service distinctive or better?
Does one have an improved delivery process or maintenance, etc?

Once you list this stuff, you'll then incorporate them into your sales and selling method. You'll develop new sales pitches, flyers, emails, or materials that may mirror your Unique Selling Price.

If you wish to explore Unique Selling Prices even additional, we have a tendency to detail tips to assist you outline yours during this article.

□ Consider Your Audience

A strong Unique Selling Price is one that cuts through the middle of our everyday lives. It's reaching the correct folks and catching their attention. It’s not broad and trying to achieve everybody.

To reach your audience, you would like to outline your niche. However, to outline your niche, you've got to appear at your audience.

Research your client base to find their interests, frustrations, desires, communication vogue, and everything else that may assist you learn additional information regarding them. It's conjointly useful to grasp things like age, gender, location, education level, and socio-economic level.

Here’s what you ought to consider :

Who is your target audience?
What area unit their needs?
Are their desires being met?
How will your product or service meet their needs?
How are you able to attract their values in your messaging?
You may have done this at the beginning of your business, however it’s smart to examine this frequently to notice any changes in interests that you simply ought to be conscious of.

9

HOW TO ENCLOSE YOUR DEALS

1. Skip The Script OR Not The Script

Part of creating your publicity feel new once more would possibly mean ditching the script. You're not a telemarketer, you're a salesman. Simply because one pitch worked on an occasion doesn't mechanically mean it'll work on ensuring you have got to grasp your audience and learn to tailor the spoken communication once necessary.

To script or to not script is fodder for abundant discussion nowadays. Whereas I agree that you simply can't use constant pitch, constant language, constant angle, etc. For each prospect you contact, there are benefits with victimization written notes including:

- Keeping you higher ready.
- Organizing your electronic messaging.
- Making you sound a lot of assured.
- Helping you keep in mind pain points.
- Improving however you overcome objections.

Some of the US can merely keep bulleted lists of pain points, benefits, and answers to objections ahead folks once job. If you choose to use a script, you ought to ne'er browse your script throughout a prospecting decision. You'll sound meretricious and robotic.

2. Uncover Their Desires

Stop performing arts around and raise the prospects of what their desires are. If you aren't certain however your product fits their desires, go back to the fundamentals and do a lot of schoolwork before job or programming a gathering. You can't enclose the deal if you don't uncover the client's desires.

Just keep in mind that typically the final word would be troublesome to uncover. For instance, once merchandising ATMs to banks, you would possibly be told by the banker that the bank is trying to find an Associate in Nursing ATM that's a lot more reliable than the previous machine they presently have. However is that the final word would be of the bank?

Doesn't the bank have the final word to attract a lot of customers and deposits?

There are innumerable ATM vendors which will show however their machines are a lot more reliable than older machines. However if your machine will do this and facilitate the bank attracting new customers, then you'll stand out.

3. Be Grateful

One of the foremost necessary reminders of all; be grateful for each chance you have got to talk with a consumer. Whether it's an associate in nursing email response, a 30-second voicemail that you simply need to come, or a sit-down strike meeting, you want to impart them with his or her time and acknowledge that they need a busy schedule. Build the meeting or courtesy decision to stand out.

4. Grasp Once To Prevent Talking

Don't harm the rapport you're attempting to make by dominating spoken communication. Let your prospects share their aspect of the story. Grasp once to square pat and perceive that a less is a lot of approach to talking will usually spark curiosity from an occasion.

Taking this a step more, keep in mind that a consumer can sell themselves on a plan long before you sell them together with your words. Lead the spoken communication to a degree wherever the consumer is asked, "How does one see this answer poignant your situation?" Then, allow them to declare themselves.

5. Don't Bash The Competition

It's not your job to attack the competition; your job is to sell your company's vision and worth. Anytime you are trying to discredit everything an occasion brings up concerning the competition, you're golf shot the prospect on the defensive. All that will produce an associate in a nursing uncomfortable scenario.

What if your competitive info isn't accurate? Currently, you've lost credibility and improved your competitor's position. it'd be best to only give your consumer with a listing of necessary queries that they must be asking all suitors, while not naming your competitors. These queries would facilitate the consumer uncovering the dirt on your competitors on their own.

6. Raise Concerning Their Budget

If you've established a true would like, and you recognize their pain points, you ought to have already connected a price to every pain purpose. If you elicit their budget at this point, (assuming they provide you an honest answer) the budget is well below your minimum charge, you ought to march on. You've lost this one. However, if you show throughout your presentation what proportion price your answer could give the consumer, you'll facilitate them see however unsuitable the budget range truly is.

7. Champion Your Product

In the past I actually have detected that no prospect can get from you if you don't grasp your product within and out. You want to be well-versed in everything your product will do. It's as easy as that.

With the complexities of a number of the products out there, this can be an associate in nursing daunting tips for anyone. I say, learn the maximum amount as your sales coaching has provided, however don't sweat it if you don't grasp one thing trivial (What proportion of Aluminum alloy is your product created with?). Simply acknowledge that it's an excellent question, grasp wherever to urge that answer, and obtain the solution back to the consumer as quickly as attainable.

8. Reference Your Coaching

All winning sales coaching programs give resources for the team to reference when the particular sales coaching session. Benefits of those tools. If your company offers a library of off-the-peg videos, take the time to rewatch key courses.

www.ingramcontent.com/pod-product-compliance
Lightning Source LLC
LaVergne TN
LVHW020524160826
845677LV00015B/3886

* 9 7 9 8 8 4 6 8 9 3 8 5 6 *